Speak Softly of Christmas

speak softly of Christmas

Poems by

JOHN CAMPBELL

EXPOSITION PRESS   **NEW YORK**

FOR LYNN
—because
when others left
you stayed
to speak softly of Christmas.

First Edition

Contents

Preface

Year follows year in the great and repetitious race toward an uncertain future. By December 31, summer sun is hardly discernible from winter wind, in recalling the past twelve months.

I find some warmth in knowing each year ends with Christmas:

A time when tenderness prevails more frequently—when gentleness surprises me even in the sullen Scrooges I have come to know—and when I may speak softly and in silence of those loves who shared some Christmases with me.

Speak Softly of Christmas is perhaps as repetitious as Christmas itself and every bit as real, its message meant at first for only three. It was written for one who never really understood, shared with one who understood and fled, and finally given in its fullness to one who stayed to understand.

I share it now with you—that you may in turn share it with someone you love; so that—in June as well as in December —this book may speak for you—softly and of Christmas.

John Campbell

PART I
Speak Softly of Christmas

ONE

Speak softly of Christmas
    secure and peaceful shelter-place
    for all who daily flee
    (across each changing calendar)
    a world gone wild with haste.

Talk tenderly of trees
    all laden with lights,
    and gaze with new understanding
    at this amazing season's stars
    which did not linger in the night
    last time you raised your eyes.

Whisper wonderingly of such a season
    that causes the shepherd
    find joy in tending flocks
    that bored him yesterday
    and promises of love to come,
    ushered in on wings of hymns
    with the crisp and cold December wind.

Speak softly of Christmas;
    it is yours and mine;
    and should it slip away unspoken of,
    through the snowbanks of idle silence
    or the canyons of too-loud conversation,
    we'll have another year to wait
    before we speak again.

So speak softly of Christmas.

TWO

I am not a king
(no matter how you stretch the word),
nor am I a bearer
of expensive gifts of royal standard.

I am just me,
bearer of a gift of love
often lost in a year of turmoil,
but so very much my own to give
at Christmas.

Crowned with smiles
of people finding reason
to break year-old frowns
on tinsel-lighted streets,
I find I'm more than king;
I'm shepherd to those I love,
fending off the wolves of loneliness.

The world has already
too many wise-men
for this year,
each with his opinion and his pride;
I'd sooner carry back a lamb of peace
to the lonely of my Bethlehem
(in imitation of a shepherd I once knew).

I'll leave the gold of empty talk,
the frankincense of false friendship,
and the myrrh of hearts gone cold
to those who feel that's wisdom.

I'd rather be a shepherd
than a king
anytime.

THREE

Warm the winter's night
with the songs of Christmas
which your life has written
this year now past.

Hang a tender wreath of love
ever so gently
on the half-closed door
of every empty heart.

Once a year seems not enough
to offer an all too troubled world
the gift of peace
(and special stars
instead of wars
across its Christmas skies).

So make this Christmas
a year-long holiday
filled with lights in children's eyes
and the evergreen of hope
and the holly of your smile.

Warm the winter night
with the togetherness of Christmas
which our lives have found
this year now past.

Hang a tender wreath of love
ever so gently
on the open door
of a better year to come.

FOUR

(for Kathy O'Neill at Christmas)

I'll miss you more than most
this Christmas.
Last year you smiled the smile
that only lives in hearts like yours
on Christmas day.

This year you'll lie in silence
where Christmas does not come,
asleep the sleep that lingers through
the Christmases to come,
which those of us
(who've yet some Christmases to go)
search for in vain
each December twenty-fifth.

The lights of trees and strains of hymns
that occupy our Yuletide senses
will barely reach that distant hill
where you rest alone
in the quietness of death.

A paradox this seems indeed,
were it not true that you've been freed
from needing gifts or doubting creed
because the Christmas peace all need
is yours
at last.

FIVE

You are my Christmas.
You always will be, you know.

Though other loves may decorate
the tree with me,
or carol in the fresh December cold,
you'll still be there,
beloved keeper of my heart,
each silent Christmas morn.

When all the parties,
which celebrate the season
with such noisy nothingness,
have ended,
and all the unhappy, shallow smiles
have gone to troubled beds,
I'll sit alone
and watch the Christmas star,
and wish for you.

So many swift-spent years
since I first kissed you,
it seems so strange that no one knows
I love you still.

Not even you.

And though it may never be
that we will share a morning star together,
I'll hope that in that distant somewhere
where you've gone,
you'll see its light
and know with gentle longing
you are my Christmas.

SIX

Taste the tingle
of Christmas snow
on an outstretched tongue.

Smile with that contagious smile
whose epidemic spread
is such a welcome change
from the furrowed frowns
of a troubled year
now past.

Come twine your little fingers
round the roughness of my hand
and walk with me
down a symphony of streets
aglitter with a harmony
of holiday lights.

I need you at Christmas—
to feel the wonder
of the season's warmth
with me.

Because Christmas alone
is no Christmas at all.

SEVEN

The old owl,
wise and warm
beneath his frosted feathers,
stares,
wide-eyed with bewilderment,
at a new star
that did not share its brilliance
with last night's world.

Where owls may wonder,
you and I are sure.
It's Christmas,
and stars appear
in people's eyes
as well as skies
on this crisp night in December.

Comfort me with stars
and silent nights,
not only in the Yuletide,
but all year long,
when I'm more often
lost in wonder
than in wisdom.

EIGHT

Season to season,
life runs too quickly,
and turning
in our path
we wonder at the years we thought
were ours,
now only a part of the annals
of the past.

For there will dawn
a Christmas
when life will celebrate the day
without our voices lifted in song

Cherish then
those Yuletides yet remaining,
and touch each day
that weaves the Christmases
in pattern.

Love each one
as though it were the last,
to make these numbered Christmas days
reason enough
for living
the yearning years between.

NINE

The year has not been good
to me.
Lost somewhere in the tangle
of the months past,
is all the warmth I'd saved
to give you lovingly
this December twenty-fifth.

Thank you
for your patient understanding
in accepting
that my gift of love
is late in coming—
and for just being there
when I needed you
and could not say the words.

Thank you for being my Christmas
unasked.

Be my Christmas yet again
when I hopefully place
next year's calendar
on last year's wall.

TEN

Will you share
a simple Christmas tree
with me this year?

This evergreen,
a thousand times passed by,
seemed tired of people's laughter
as it reached out to me
in the cold night air.

It seemed to ask for
a coat of twinkling lights
and tinsel garlands
as had the other trees,
now long sold and carried off
to waiting cars
and bright December windows.

For six years
my little tree
had braved the wilderness,
growing in anticipation
of a Christmas yet to come,
when,
in dying,
its life would bring joy.

I could not let its hopes
of being a Christmas tree
die alone
on an empty lot
under a Christmas night sky.

And so,
though not so finely shaped,
it is my tree.

Please share my tree
in its short life
with me.

And if you find you can,
please share my life
itself.

That it too,
neglected by others
who found more to laugh at
than to admire
and love,
will at last
stand tall
in someone's eyes.

They've been so long in growing,
my tree and my life—
come take them now as yours.

And we will find
the words we need
to speak softly of Christmas.

PART II
Gently Be My Christmas

ONE

Tenderly
I watched you sleeping in the soft light
of the Christmas tree,
satisfied with the hard floor
and my shoulder for your pillow.

Too long we had shopped the tinseled windows
and blinked at holiday displays.
Then, yawning with the season's rush
and holding tight each other's hand,
we hurried out of reach
of greedy crowds
and harried mothers
prompting Santa Claus
through storefront glass.

How much more Christmas this,
the two of us alone
wrapped in garlands of thought
and warmed by the silent carols
of togetherness.

I love the way you sleep.
But mostly I love just you.

So gently be my Christmas
everyday
until December twenty-fifth
no longer lends us reason
for each year.

TWO

I love you at Christmas
but really no more
than I did
on Lincoln's birthday,
or New Year's Eve,
or two weeks ago Tuesday.

Often neglected in the rush of days,
my love thirsts
for the pine-scented
gift giving refreshment
of Christmas.

Not that I've ever loved you less
at any moment
of our being us.
I've just wasted precious moments
building futures at the expense of gazing
into the nowness
of your accepting eyes.

Christmas always bids me
see again
your timid smile
and feel unspoken messages
traced upon my lips
with gentle fingers
asking me to know you
just a little more.

Do I love you at Christmas?
If I do not
then there really is
no Santa Claus.

THREE

I waited patiently
eight Christmas years
for you
to trim my tree.

And then you did
with love lights
and ornaments of tenderness
and you.

And on that topmost branch
where even God could see,
you hung the star
I'd snatched for you
from a crisp Christmas morning sky.

My tree is bare
this winter of my life.

Come decorate its barren branches
once again,
forgiving me the year's trespasses.
For my Christmas will not be
without your soft breath against my neck
and warmth against my soul.

FOUR

The Christmas lights
I see sparkling this year
decorate not trees
or windows.
Not even children's eyes.
   Just you.

FIVE

December is tiptoeing
softly
into next year
unnoticed.

End this year with me
as my Christmas love,
held under mistletoe in warm embrace.
Let me kiss the holly of your lips,
to tell you
you are so much more
than just my holiday.

May my eyes
be so full of you
that even twinkling pine trees
flocked with snow
will not seem anything
but dull.
I will not love you less
fifty Christmases from now.
Did you know that
all through this too-swift year?
I did.

SIX

You've been my Christmas
in April
as much as in December.
I've heard the angels sing each time I kissed you.
Perhaps I am too used
to celebrating Christmas all year round.
Still, wish me Merry Christmas
as if for the first time,
well knowing you've said it wordlessly
a thousand times a day,
each time you looked at me.

SEVEN

Thank you
for sitting so close to me
each second
of that San Francisco flight,
and for your little fingers
entwined in mine.

Your body close to mine
has always said
a Christmas message
not found on any card.

Had more people on that plane
held each other
as you held me
(instead of boxes wrapped at Macy's)
maybe Christmas would have had
half a chance
to teach us how to love.

Stockings and cranberry sauce aside,
you were my Christmas
high above a gift-mad world
that cold Yuletide morning.

EIGHT

Be my Christmas star.
Though no wise man,
I'll follow you to an unknown Bethlehem.
Do not disappear
halfway to the manger of fulfillment,
or lead me to a Herod's deceit.
I helplessly accept your silent invitation
because I love you
as wise men can ill afford to do.

NINE

My mailbox
gorges itself
on Christmas cards
lately.

Most are meaningless memos
to make my memory
search
its dusty corners
to recall who it is
that belongs
to these unfamiliar names.

Thank you for not adding
to this pile of postmarks.
Our Christmas verses
are best said
in silence.

Should I ever settle
for a piece of colored paper
to be a special envoy of my love
dispatched alone,
then know
my December need for you
has died.

That will no doubt happen
the third Christmas
after never.

TEN

The Virgin Mary kneels
too awkward and too straight
in those scenes
that paint the Christmas story so unreal.
I imagine she was tired and frightened
and cuddled in her Joseph's arms.
How nice to think she needed loving too!

ELEVEN

I'd bring you presents
more exciting
were I rich.

But once again this year
I offer only poems
filled with words
and typing errors
and my love.

Perhaps someday
I'll buy you
more than dreams upon my pillow,
but no gift
that I could give you
would say more.

You are my Christmas angel.
You make Christmas worth
the wait
and the long uncertain days
between each one.

So come gently be my Christmas,
leave the partying to fools,
and just love me through the Yuletide
and the year.

PART III
A Gift of Tenderness

ONE

A gift of tenderness
is all I ask
to fill my Christmas longing;
a hand to hold
a gentle touch
a sense of still belonging.

A gift of tenderness
so rich in warmth and feeling,
your love expressed
without shallow words,
your silence as my healing.

A gathering
of gifts of gain
won't lie beneath my tree;
the failures of this
forgotten year
are all the presents there are to see.

So won't you give
the gift I need
in all its sacredness:
your heart's response,
your body's warmth,
a gift of tenderness?

I'll share my smiles,
my touch, my tears,
an end to emptiness,
if you will give at Christmas time
a gift of tenderness.

TWO

If there were a way to do so,
    I'd like to give you all the gifts
    you most desire
and add to that a Christmas gift
    of love
to tell you that I really care.

May this Christmas find you
    not only older and more learned
    than the last,
but especially wiser
    and more full
of quiet understanding.

And may the smiles and caring
    you and I have shared
    in busy avenues and quiet rooms
    these past few months ,

stay with us through many Christmases to come
    when, though we have gone
    our separate ways,
the memories of times we walked and talked
    together
will fill us up with Christmas
to last our whole life through.

THREE

Have you stood upon your Christmas hill
against a cold and star-lit winter sky
and wished a miracle
as I have?

A world festooned
with hymns and holly
makes light the shepherd's watch
over the flocks that are his tiny piece
of world.

And stirring in his silent soul
are hopes and wishes
for gifts sublime
and goals once thought unthinkable
and not beheld there yesterday.

Shepherds would be kings
if miracles were real.
And so they are at Christmas time
when every man becomes a monarch
through the miracle of love.

Perhaps this Christmas
once again
miracles will not be only toys of dreamers
but rather gifts from a God
who knows we need such things
upon a Christmas night.

FOUR

You've only been a voice to me
these past December weeks,
pleasant
but not quite human,
your "youness" lost somewhere
in the tangle of telephone lines.

Your name's Michelle
and that is all I'm told
besides the multitude of messages
you've gathered all day long
to hand me at the close of day
(most often more anxieties
than joys).

A moment more than is required
a word
a laugh
a gentle word
would be a gift
I'd cherish for this Christmas
soon to come.

But in a world where business
binds us all,
we've neither thought nor time
for tenderness and warmth.

How sad.

Were I not so shy,
I'd like to tell you
of my need to know you
and to celebrate a Christmas every day,
and how your voice alone
could make it so.

FIVE

This trying year
has grown around me
like a tree too seldom pruned;
those who know my name
now number in the thousands,
and yet I wonder where exists
one who knows me past my name.

This trying year
of subtle changes
has seen me smile too often at faceless crowds
shadowed beyond cold stage lights;
how did I come to stand
before untouchable multitudes
when really all I asked
was one to touch
even when the poetry was gone?

This trying year
has taught me that success is often failure
and failure sometimes a success;
but putting both aside,
I move in swift anticipation
toward the place I yearly hide with hope
and walk with peace
and stay with gentleness.

This trying year
is finally drawing to its stormy end,
but not before I've had my Christmas Day
to make all wrong things
right again.

SIX

The Christmases I might have had
sleep on
in that eternal sleep
of those who've lost their chance
in bidding to become reality.

Had loves not gone
or some love softly come
to take me down some different road
than the one I find I'm on,
what twinkling tree
would stand this Christmas in the window,
and whose window would it be?

Christmas past is Christmas not to be,
and Christmas yet to come gives life to hope;
but Christmas days that might have been
but never were
lend nourishment to thoughts of joys
that might have been.

I'm greedy in my need for Christmas trees.
I'll take those now at hand
and still wish for those
that never grew.

The same with loves.

So bear with me,
my love of Christmas Present,
in my strange ways
of longing for past Yuletides
and those yet to come
and also those that never were
or yet will be.
I love you none the less
because of this.

The poet who has come to live
within me
must try transcending
past and future both,
as if to find some Christmas waiting somewhere
that is his now
and then
and his all that might have been:
a universal wreath of Christmas wealth.

So touch my hand
and press your December kisses to my lips;
come sing the warmth of this year's Christmas
with the carols of yesterday.

Whatever might have been
will always be a part of me;
but you are just as much my Christmas
as that will ever be.

SEVEN

Freeways are my Christmas trees
shimmering with red and white
of thousands of twinkling bulbs
in the cold December night.

Come ride my Christmas tree with me
and tell me that it pleases you
to see my Christmas lights
—and be one too!!!

EIGHT

You've stepped on my tender toes
and kicked my soft shins unknowingly
and poked me in the eye
with those monstrous packages
as we pressed together
out of necessity
in our overpopulated elevator.

I've always favored closeness,
but of another kind.

On you go
to buy, wrap and send
with a certain emptiness
that makes these long hours
nothing short of wasted
in buying someone else's handiwork
to tell the ones you love
what should be said
with kisses and with smiles.

But I suppose the war you wage
against the thousand other gift-mad warriors
invading this dollar-mad shopping mall
still does say something of love.

I wish you'd take a Christmas minute
just to gaze at me
—to reach out with your pretty eyes
and touch me with your Christmas smile.

I'd like to make you drop those silly packages
and take your little hand in mine
and make you run away with me.

I'd show you Christmas trees
still living on the hill
with bird's nests as their ornaments
and trimmed with stars instead of
store-bought lights.

This is your floor,
and as you push your perilous path
from out the elevator's captive crowd,
you look at me with some suspicion
of my smile.

I wish you'd loved me too,
if only for those brief December moments
between floors
when all we had was each other
in a crowded corner to ourselves.
Christmas spirit may be hanging heavy
on counters and colorful display racks,
but somewhere we have failed
in bringing the Season's warmth
into elevators where we face each other
in a naked silence.

I didn't even know your name,
but I loved you
and wished you Merry Christmas
in my heart.

NINE

Gift me with your smile.
That would be enough of Christmas
to warm a weary winter's night
and carry me on
to many a Christmas yet to come.

Gift me with your surprise visit
in the darkness of this Season's quiet night;
your gentle knock upon my lonely door
(long since abandoned by the friendly fists
of former friends)
would be enough
to make my spirit rise again
to listen for the sound of angels' wings.

Gift me with your smile
at Christmas time
that I may find a stable of shelter
in my unfriendly Bethlehem
away from a world growing colder every year
and close to the warmth of you.

Gift me with your smile
and you will give me Christmas
as it's never been.

Please.

Gift me with your smile.

TEN

Graze safely
in the winter night's stillness,
sheep of my charge.

Whatever former fears
of wolves and darkness
were yours and mine
have passed forever now.

Tonight,
in the sleeping city,
resting securely and unaware,
the questions of searching centuries
lie answered in a mother's tender arms.

Not in the glories of war,
nor in the passions of politics,
but in the simple hymn of birth
has come the final fulfillment
of prophecies
forgotten in the frayed and weary years.

So graze safely
in the winter night's stillness,
sheep of my charge.

Whatever former fear
of wolves and darkness
was yours and mine
has passed forever now
in the joyous rush of angels' wings
heralding the hope
of this first Christmas night.

ELEVEN

I need a million dollars' worth
of Christmas smiles,
a small bag of crimson tears,
and a long life to mix them in.

I need a diamond cluster
of Christmas stars,
your sky to set them in,
and a life of nights
to give them all to you.

I need a Christmas sunrise
that never turns to day,
and a Christmas sunset that never really fades,
and you
breathing gently next to me.

I need a thousand words to speak for me,
and a world of Christmas silence
to echo thoughts unsaid,
and your eyes saying
you know
what I feel.

I need a million dollars' worth
of Christmas smiles,
a small bag of crimson tears,
and a long life to mix them in.

TWELVE

(for Suzanne)

We've decorated
eight years of Christmas trees
together.
We've laughed our crowded way
through stores and shops
in search of gifts
that best said "I love you so."
We've spoken softly words
of Christmas closeness,
even in the midst of summer time,
and then one Christmas held on tightly
when you nearly died.

Christmas belongs to us
if it belongs to anyone,
and so I've told you
every year
in poems meant for you
though read by other eyes
who could never understand
that I was emptiness without you.

And so you'll understand
if I am silent
this Christmas
when you've chosen other ways
to celebrate this universal day of loving
and to fill your winter nights
with another's warmth.

If go you must,
then come at least and kiss me
and wish me MERRY CHRISTMAS
in the best way that you can
to make up for the years
when all my gifts will be memories of you
and every hymn but your name
echoing in my heart.

THIRTEEN

I awoke from a dream of you
this December morning
and suddenly
it was Christmas
as it never was before.

Every wish of peace and joy
that surrounds this sentimental season,
had disappeared from inside
every Christmas card
and lay warmly in your arms.

I awoke from a dream of you
this December morning
and suddenly
it was Christmas
as it never was before.

FOURTEEN

The surface of the street
is cracked and old now,
and the window pane I pressed
against my little nose
in looking at what I then thought
was the world
belongs to a house much older
and much sadder
than the one the boy in me had known.

Christmas once lived in this house
as it would never live again
in all those other places
and all those other times
that would slowly break
my Christmas dream
into reality.
Christmas once lived here.

FIFTEEN

If this be my last Christmas,
let me spend it here with you
in the warmth of understanding
that I find in very few.

Keep away the frowning faces
of those who criticize my dreams
because they've misplaced all their own
and forgotten what Christmas means.
If this be my last Christmas
let me spend it here with you
in the love and tenderness of one
who knows that dreams come true.

SIXTEEN

Christmas is coming
            And on a Monday too
Coloring that day white for once
            Instead of its normal blue
Are Christmases
            And Mondays
                Compatible??

SEVENTEEN

I'll wait with hope
this Christmas Eve
for you to be my gift
of laughter and stillness
of pleasure and pain
of morning and sunsets
of sunshine and rain;
but most of all
I beg of you
be
my gift of tenderness.

EIGHTEEN

My heaven is to love you;
there is no greater fullfilment
here
or hereafter.
I know that now.

What was emptiness in me
is full now—of you.
Scattered fragments of my once sure life
fit easily together once again
in a simple reconstruction
of the broken smiles of yesterday.

That you do not know I love you
matters but minutely.
I wish you only joy
and the completeness of your dreams.
To ask that you, in turn, love me
would be a selfish thought indeed
that well might shatter
yet again
the glued and replaced pieces of my heart.

I love you secretly,
and that should be enough for any man
athirst for something gentle
in a world which places thorns
even on roses.

If I can watch you
move in softness
and smile in serenity
from time to time—
If I can hear you singing
the symphony of happiness
and speak of joys you've found—

If I can take you tenderly
and make your body's warmth the warmth of mine
but once in a life of years—
then I will be completely complete,
for your being one with me
would make *my* being me
so much easier to be.

And if, by chance,
some lost and long-time coming day,
you turn your gentle eyes on me,
and find, without my asking,
that you might love me too,
then a promised paradise
will be a disappointing reward
and fade in the fullness
of you.

For you are all a promise ever promised,
and every spring that thawed a winter's cold.
Words fall defeated in their purpose
as they lamely lisp the thoughts
of what you are
to what I am.

I dare not risk the wish
even in the secret and peaceful forests
of my mind
that someday you might touch the tallness
of the tree of my hopes
and love me as I love you.

I will lie down nightly with my solitude
and be at peace.

For my heaven is to love you,
and the greatest of my gifts
to hear your gentle voice
speak softly of Christmas.